Gerald Scarfe

THE WALL

WRITTEN AND DIRECTED BY ROGER WATERS

PERFORMED BY

PINK FLOYD

ROGER WATERS · DAVID GILMOUR · NICK MASON · RICHARD WRIGHT

WITH

ANDY BOWN BASS SNOWY WHITE GUITAR

WILLIE WILSON DRUMS PETER WOODS KEYBOARDS

BACKING VOCALS

JOHN JOYCE · JIM FARBER · STAN HAAS · JOE CHEMAY

MUSICAL DIRECTOR — DAVID GILMOUR

ART DIRECTION — GERALD SCARFE

SOUND MIXING — JAMES GUTHRIE

ANIMATION DESIGN AND DIRECTION — GERALD SCARFE

ASST. ANIMATION DIRECTOR : MICHAEL STUART ASST. ART DIRECTOR : JILL BROOKS.

ANIMATION : MICHAEL STUART · BILL HAGEE. GREG MILLER · CHIS CAUNTER TRACE + PAINT : SANDY HOUSTON

EDITING : TONY FISH · PETER HEARN · CAMERA : JULIEN HOLDAWAY · RICHARD WOLFF PRODUCTION SUPVR LANCE PAUL

SOUND BY

BRITTANIA ROW AUDIO INC.

ROBBIE WILLIAMS

SETH GOLDMAN

NIGEL TAYLOR

WITH THANKS TO

STANLEY MILLER

JERRY BRADLEY

ROBIN FOX

SANDRA MC IN TOSH

PHIL TAYLOR — STAGE EQUIPMENT ·

LIGHTING AND SPECIAL EFFECTS

BRITTANIA ROW LIGHTING INC

GRAHAM FLEMING

MARK FISHER

DON JOCE

MICK TREADWELL

ROCKY PAULSON

WITH THANKS TO

JONATHAN PARK

ROSIE BAILLIE

ANDY SHIELDS · PROJECTIONIST

WORDS AND MUSIC BY ROGER WATERS EXCEPT

YOUNG LUST (WATERS GILMOUR) COMFORTABLY NUMB (GILMOUR WATERS)

RUN LIKE HELL (GILMOUR WATERS) THE TRIAL (WATERS EZRIN)

SPECIAL THANKS TO NORMAN LAWRENCE

PINK FLOYD MANAGEMENT · STEVE O'ROURKE E·M·K·A· PRODUCTIONS

Gerald Scarfe

In the Flesh?

So ya
Thought ya
Might like to go to the show
To feel the warm thrill of confusion
That space cadet glow
Tell me is something eluding you sunshine?
Is this not what you expected to see?
If you'd like to find out what's behind these cold eyes?
You'll just have to claw your way through the
Disguise

The Thin Ice

Mamma loves her baby
And daddy loves you too
And the sea may look warm to you babe
And the sky may look blue
But Ooooh babe
Ooooh baby blue
Ooooh babe
If you should go skating
On the thin ice of modern life
Dragging behind you the silent reproach
Of a million tear stained eyes
Don't be surprised, when a crack in the ice
Appears under your feet
You slip out of your depth and out of your mind
With your fear flowing out behind you
As you claw the thin ice

Another Brick in the Wall. part 1.

Daddy's flown across the ocean
Leaving just a memory
A Snap shot in the family album
Daddy what else did you leave for me
Daddy what d'ya leave behind for me
All in all it was just a brick in the wall
All in all it was all just bricks in the wall.

The Happiest Days of our Lives

When we grew up and went to school
There were certain teachers who would
Hurt the children anyway they could
By pouring their derision
Upon anything we did
And exposing every weakness
However carefully hidden by the kids
But in the town it was well known
When they got home at night, their fat and
Psychopathic wives would thrash them
Within inches of their lives

Another Brick in the Wall part 2

We don't need no education
We don't need no thought control
No dark sarcasm in the classroom
Teachers leave the kids alone,
Hey teacher leave us kids alone
All in all its just another brick in the wall
All in all you're just another brick in the wall

Mother

Mother do you think they'll drop the bomb
Mother do you think they'll like the song
Mother do you think they'll try to break my balls
Mother should I build a wall
Mother should I run for president
Mother should I trust the government
Mother will they put me in the firing line
Mother am I really dying.
Hush now baby don't you cry
Mama's gonna make all of your
Nightmares come true
Mamas gonna put all of her fears into you
mamas gonna keep you right here
Under her wing
She won't let you fly but she might let you sing
Mama will keep baby cosy and warm
Ooooh Babe Ooooh Babe Ooooh Babe
Of course Mam'll help build the wall

Mother do you think she's good enough for me
Mother do you think she's dangerous to me
Mother will she tear your little boy apart
Mother will she break my heart.

Hush now baby, baby don't you cry
mama's gonna check out all your girl friends for y
Mama won't let anyone dirty get through
mama's gonna wait up till you come in
mama will always find out where
You've been
Mama's gonna keep you healthy and clean
Ooooh Babe Ooooh Babe Ooooh Babe
You'll always be a baby to me
Mother, did it need to be so high.

Goodbye Blue Sky

Oooooooooooooooooh
Did you see the frightened ones
Did you hear the falling bombs
Did you ever wonder
Why we had to run for shelter
When the promise of a brave new world
Unfurled beneath a clear blue sky
Oooooooooooooooooooh
Did you see the frightened ones
Did you hear the falling bombs
The flames are all long gone
But the pain lingers on
Goodbye Blue Sky
Goodbye Blue Sky
Goodbye

Empty Spaces / What shall we do now ?

What shall we use to fill the empty
Spaces where we used to talk
How shall I fill the final places
How shall I complete the wall

Shall we buy a new guitar
Shall we drive a more powerful car
Shall we work straight through the night
Shall we get into fights
Leave the lights on
Drop bombs
Do tours of the East
Contract diseases
Bury bones
Break up homes
Send flowers by phone
Take to drink
Go to shrinks
Give up meat
Rarely sleep
Keep people as pets
Train dogs
Race rats
Fill the attic with cash
Bury treasure
Store up leisure
But never relax at all
With our backs to the wall

Gerald Scarfe

Young Lust

I am just a new boy
A stranger in this town
Where are all the good times?
Who's gonna show this stranger around?
Who? Who? Who? Who?
Ooooooooh I need a dirty woman
Oooooooh I need a dirty girl
Will some cold woman in this desert land
Make me feel like a real man
Take this rock and roll refugee
Oooh Babe set me free
Oooh, Oooh, Oooh, Oooh
Ooooooooh I need a dirty woman
Oooooooh I need a dirty girl.

One of my turns

Day after day, love turns grey
Like the skin of a dying man
Night after night, we pretend it's all right
But I have grown older and
You have grown colder and
Nothing is very much fun any more.

And I can feel one of my turns coming on.
I feel, cold as a razor blade
Tight as a tourniquet
Dry as a funeral drum,
Run to the bedroom, in the suitcase on the left
You'll find my favourite axe
Don't look! so frightened
This is just a passing phase
Just one of my bad days.
Would you like to watch T.V.?
Or get between the sheets?
Or contemplate the silent freeway?
Would you like something to eat?
Would you like to learn to fly?
Would you like to see me try?
Would you like to call the cops?
Do you think it's time I stopped?
Why are you running away??

Don't Leave me now

Ooooh Babe
Don't leave me now.
Don't say it's the end of the road
Remember the flowers I sent
I need you Babe
To put through the shredder
In front of my friends
Ooooh Babe
Don't leave me now?
How could you go?
When you know how I need you
To beat to a pulp on a Saturday night
Ooooh Babe
Don't leave me now
How can you treat me this way
Running away
I need you Babe
Why are you running away?
Oooooh Babe!

Another Brick in the Wall part 3

I don't need no arms around me
I don't need no drugs to calm me
I have seen the writing on the wall
Don't think I'll need anything at all
No don't think I'll need anything at all
All in All it was all just bricks in the wall
All in All you were all just bricks in the wall

Goodbye Cruel World

Goodbye cruel world
I'm leaving you today
Goodbye
Goodbye
Goodbye
Goodbye all you people
There's nothing you can say
to make me change
my mind
Goodbye.

Hey you

Hey you! out there in the cold
Getting lonely, getting old, can you feel me
Hey you! standing in the aisles
With itchy feet and fading smiles, can you feel me
Hey you! don't help them to bury the light
Don't give in without a fight.
Hey you! out there on your own
Sitting naked by the phone would you touch me
Hey you! with your ear against the wall
Waiting for someone to call out would you touch me
Hey you! would you help me to carry the stone
Open your heart, I'm coming home
But it was only fantasy
The wall was too high, as you can see
No matter how he tried he could not break free
And the worms ate into his brain
Hey you! out there on the road
Doing what you're told, can you help me
Hey you! out there beyond the wall
Breaking bottles in the hall, can you help me
Hey you! don't tell me there's no hope at all
Together we stand, divided we fall.

Is there anybody out there?

Is there anybody out there?

Nobody Home

I've got a little black book with my poems in
I've got a bag with a toothbrush and a comb in
When I'm a good dog they sometimes throw me a bone in
I got elastic bands keeping my shoes on
Got those swollen hand blues
Got thirteen channels of shit on the T.V. to choose from
I've got electric light
And I've got second sight
I've got amazing powers of observation
And that is how I know
When I try to get through
On the telephone to you
There'll be nobody home
I've got the obligatory Hendrix perm
And the inevitable pinhole burns
All down the front of my favourite satin shirt
I've got nicotine stains on my fingers
I've got a silver spoon on a chain
I've got a grand piano to prop up my mortal remains
I've got wild staring eyes
I've got a strong urge to fly
But I've got nowhere to fly to
Ooooh Babe when I pick up the phone
There's still nobody home
I've got a pair of Gohills boots
And I've got fading roots.

Vera

Does anybody here remember Vera Lynn
Remember how she said that
We would meet again
Some sunny day
Vera! Vera!
What has become of you
Does anybody else in here
Feel the way I do.

Bring the boys back home

Bring the boys back home
Bring the boys back home
Don't leave the children on their own
Bring the boys back home

Comfortably Numb

Hello,
Is there anybody in there
Just nod if you can hear me
Is there anyone at home
Come on now
I hear you're feeling down
I can ease your pain
And get you on your feet again
Relax
I'll need some information first
Just the basic facts
Can you show me where it hurts.

There is no pain, you are receding
A distant ship smoke on the horizon
You are only coming through in waves
Your lips move but I can't hear what you're saying
When I was a child I had a fever
My hands felt just like two balloons
Now I've got that feeling once again
I can't explain, you would not understand
This is not how I am
I have become comfortably numb

O.K.
Just a little pin prick
There'll be no more aaaaaaaah!
But you may feel a little sick
Can you stand up?
I do, believe it's working, good
That'll keep you going through the show
Come on it's time to go.
There is no pain, you are receding
A distant ship smoke on the horizon
You are only coming through in waves
Your lips move but I can't hear what you're saying
When I was a child
I caught a fleeting glimpse
Out of the corner of my eye
I turned to look but it was gone
I cannot put my finger on it now
The child is grown
The dream is gone
And I have become
Comfortably numb

The Show must go on.

Oooh Ma Oooh Pa
Does the show have to go on
Oooh Pa take me home
Oooh Ma let me go
Do I have to stand up
Wild eyed in the spotlight
What a nightmare Why
Don't I turn and run
There must be some mistake
I didn't mean to let them
Take away my soul
Am I too old is it too late
Oooh Ma Oooh Pa
Where has the feeling gone?
Oooh Ma Oooh Pa?
Will I remember the songs?
The show must go on.

Gerald Scarfe

Waiting for the worms.

Ooooh You cannot reach me now
Ooooh No matter how you try
Goodbye cruel world it's over
Walk on by
Sitting in a bunker here behind my wall
Waiting for the worms to come
In perfect isolation here behind my wall
Waiting for the worms to come
Waiting to cut out the deadwood
Waiting to clean up the city
Waiting to follow the worms
Waiting to put on a black shirt
Waiting to weed out the weaklings
Waiting to smash in their windows
And kick in their doors.

Waiting for the final solution
To strengthen the strain
Waiting to follow the worms
Waiting to turn on the showers
And fire the ovens
Waiting for the queers and the coons
and the reds and the Jews
Waiting to follow the worms
Would you like to see Britannia
Rule again my friend
All you have to do is follow the worms
Would you like to send our coloured cousins
Home again my friend
All you need to do is follow the worms.

Stop

Stop
I wanna go home
Take off this uniform
And leave the show
And I'm waiting in this cell
Because I have to know
Have I been guilty all this time

In the Flesh

So ya
Thought ya
Might like to
Go to the show
To feel the warm thrill of confusion
That space cadet glow
I've got some bad news for you sunshine
Pink isn't well he stayed back at the hotel
And they sent us along as a surrogate band
And we're going to find out where you fans
Really stand
Are there any queers in the theatre tonight
Get 'em up against the wall
There's one in the spotlight
He don't look right to me
Get him up against the wall
That one looks Jewish
And that one's a coon
Who let all this riff raff into the room
There's one smoking a joint and
Another with spots
If I had my way
I'd have all of you shot

Run like Hell.

You better run like hell
You better make your face up in
Your favourite disguise
With your button down lips and your
Roller blind eyes
With your empty smile
And your hungry heart
Feel the bile rising from your guilty past
With your nerves in tatters
When the cockleshell shatters
And the hammers batter
Down the door
You better run like hell
You better run all day
And run all night
And keep your dirty feelings
Deep inside. And if you
Take your girlfriend
Out tonight,
You better park the car
Well out of sight
'Cos if they catch you in the back seat
Trying to pick her locks
They're gonna send you back to mother
In a cardboard box
You better run.

The Trial
Good morning Worm your honour
The crown will plainly show
The prisoner who now stands before you
Was caught red handed showing feelings
Showing feelings of an almost human nature
Shame on him
This will not do
Call the schoolmaster
I always said he'd come to no good
In the end your honour
If they'd let me have my way I could
Have flayed him into shape
But my hands were tied
The bleeding hearts and artists
Let him get away with murder
Let me hammer him today
Crazy toys in the attic I am crazy
They must have taken my marbles away
Call the defendants wife
You little shit, you're in it now
I hope they throw away the key
You should have talked to me more often
Than you did, but no you had to
Go your own way. Have you broken any
Homes up lately?
"Just five minutes Worm your honour
Him and me alone
Babe
Come to mother baby let me hold you
In my arms
M'lud I never wanted him to
Get in any trouble
Why'd he ever have to leave me
Worm your honour let me take him home
Crazy over the rainbow I am crazy
Bars in the window
There must have been a door there in the wall
When I came in
Crazy over the rainbow he is crazy
The evidence before the court is
Incontravertable, there's no need for
The jury to retire
In all my years of judging
I have never heard before
Of someone more deserving
The full penalty of law
The way you made them suffer
Your exquisite wife and mother
Fills me with the urge to defecate
But my friend you have revealed your
Deepest fear
I sentance you to be exposed before
Your peers
Tear down the wall.
Gerald Scarfe

Gerald Scarfe

Outside the Wall
All alone, or in twos
The ones who really love you
Walk up and down outside the wall
Some hand in hand
Some gathering together in bands
The bleeding hearts and artists
Make their stand
And when they've given you their all
Some stagger and fall, after all it's not easy
Banging your heart against some mad buggers
Wall

Pink Floyd The Wall

In the Flesh?

Words & Music by
ROGER WATERS

Slowly

D
A
space ca-det glow.
Tell me is some-thing e-lud-ing you sun-shine?
Bm
E7
C♯m
Is this not what you ex-pect-ed to see? If you want to find out what's be-hind these cold eyes, You'll
E
A
just have to claw your way through this dis-guise.
D
A
D
A
D
A
E
A
rall.

The Thin Ice

Words & Music by
ROGER WATERS

C Am Fmaj7 G
Drag-ging on be-hind you the sil-ent re-proach— Of a mil-li-on —— tear stained eyes. ——
C Am F G
Don't be sur-prised— when a crack in the ice —— Ap-pears un-der your feet. —— You slip
C Em Am F G
out of your depth and out of your mind— With your fear flow-ing out be-hind you As you claw the thin ice.
No Chord Am No Chord
ff
Am No chord D G C

Another Brick in the Wall. part 1.

Words & Music by
ROGER WATERS

in the fam - 'ly al — bum.
Dad-dy, — what else — did you leave — for me? —
G
Gm
ff
Dad-dy, what d'ya leave be-hind— for me?
Dm
mf
F
C
All in all — it was just a brick in the

Dm
F
wall.
All in all—
C
Dm
— it was all just bricks in the wall.

C
Dm
B♭
C
F
Dm

Am
Dm
fade -

The Happiest Days of our Lives

Words & Music by
ROGER WATERS

F
Am
pour-ing their de-ri-sion—Up-on any-thing— we did— Ex-pos-ing ev-'ry weak-ness How-
Em
Am
ev-er care—ful-ly hid-den by the kids.
D
But in— the town it was well known When they got
B♭
Gm
C7
home at night Their fat and psy-cho-path-ic wives would thrash them-With-in inch-es of their lives.
F
B♭
F

Another Brick in the Wall, part 2

Words and Music by
ROGER WATERS

Tea - cher, leave them kids a - lone.
Tea - chers, leave the kids a - lone.
G
Hey, teacher! Leave them kids alone!
Hey, teacher! Leave us kids alone!
Dm
Am
G
F
C
Dm
All in all it's just an - oth-er brick in the wall.
All in all you're just an - oth-er brick in the wall.
F
C
Dm
All in all you're just an - oth- er brick in the wall.
All in all you're just an - oth- er brick in the wall.

1
2
Dm
fade
silence

Mother

Words & Music by
ROGER WATERS

C
G
Moth-er, do you think they'll try— to break— my balls?
D
C
Ooh
Ah, Moth-er, should I build the wall?—
G
Moth-er, should I run for pres— i - dent?
C
D
G
Moth-er, should I trust the gov— ern - ment?
C

D
G
C
Moth - er, will they put me in — the fir—— ing line?
G
D
C
Ooh,
Ah, is it just a waste of time?——
G
G
Hush now, ba—by, ba—— by, don't you
C
cry.
F
C
Ma - ma's gon-na make all of your night-mares come true
Ma - ma's gon-na check out all your girl-friends for you,

F C F C
Ma-ma's gon-na put all of her fears in-to you, Ma-ma's gon-na keep you right here un-der her wing. She
Ma-ma won't—let an-y-one dir-ty get through, Ma-ma's— gon-na wait up un-til you get in.
F C F C
won't let you fly but she might let you sing, Ma-ma's gon-na keep ba-by cos-y and
Ma-ma will al-ways find out where you've been, Ma-ma's gon-na keep ba-by health-y and
G D C D C TO CODA
warm.
clean.
Ooh babe,— ooh babe,—
D C G C
Ooh babe, of course Ma-ma's gon-na help build the wall.
G C G

C
D
C
G
C
G
Moth - er, do you think she's good— e -
C
C
G
nough
for me?
Moth - er, do you think she's dan— ger -
C
G
ous
to me? —

C
Moth-er, will she tear your lit— tle boy— a -
G
part?
D
Ooh,
C
G
D. 𝄋 al 𝄌
Ah, moth-er, will she break my heart? ——
CODA 𝄌
D
C
G
Ooh babe, you'll al- ways be a ba - by to me.
C
Moth-er, did it need to be— so high?
rall. . . . .

Goodbye Blue Sky

Words & Music by
ROGER WATERS

D
Bm
Ooh
Am
B/A
Did, did, did, did you see the fright-ened ones?
Am
B/A
To Coda
Am
Did, did, did, did you hear the fall-ing bombs?
Did, did, did, did you ev-er
B/A
Am
A7
D
A
D
won-der Why we had to run for shel-ter When the prom-ise of a brave new world Un-furled be-neath a
Bm
D
D. 𝄋 al 𝄌
clear blue sky? —

CODA
Am
B
The flames are all long gone — But the pain — lin - gers on. —
D
A7/D
G
D
Good - bye, — Blue Sky, —
A7/D
G
D
Am/D
Good - bye, — Blue Sky, — Good-bye,
D
Am/D
Good - bye.
No Chord
fade

Empty Spaces / What shall we do now ?

Words & Music by
ROGER WATERS

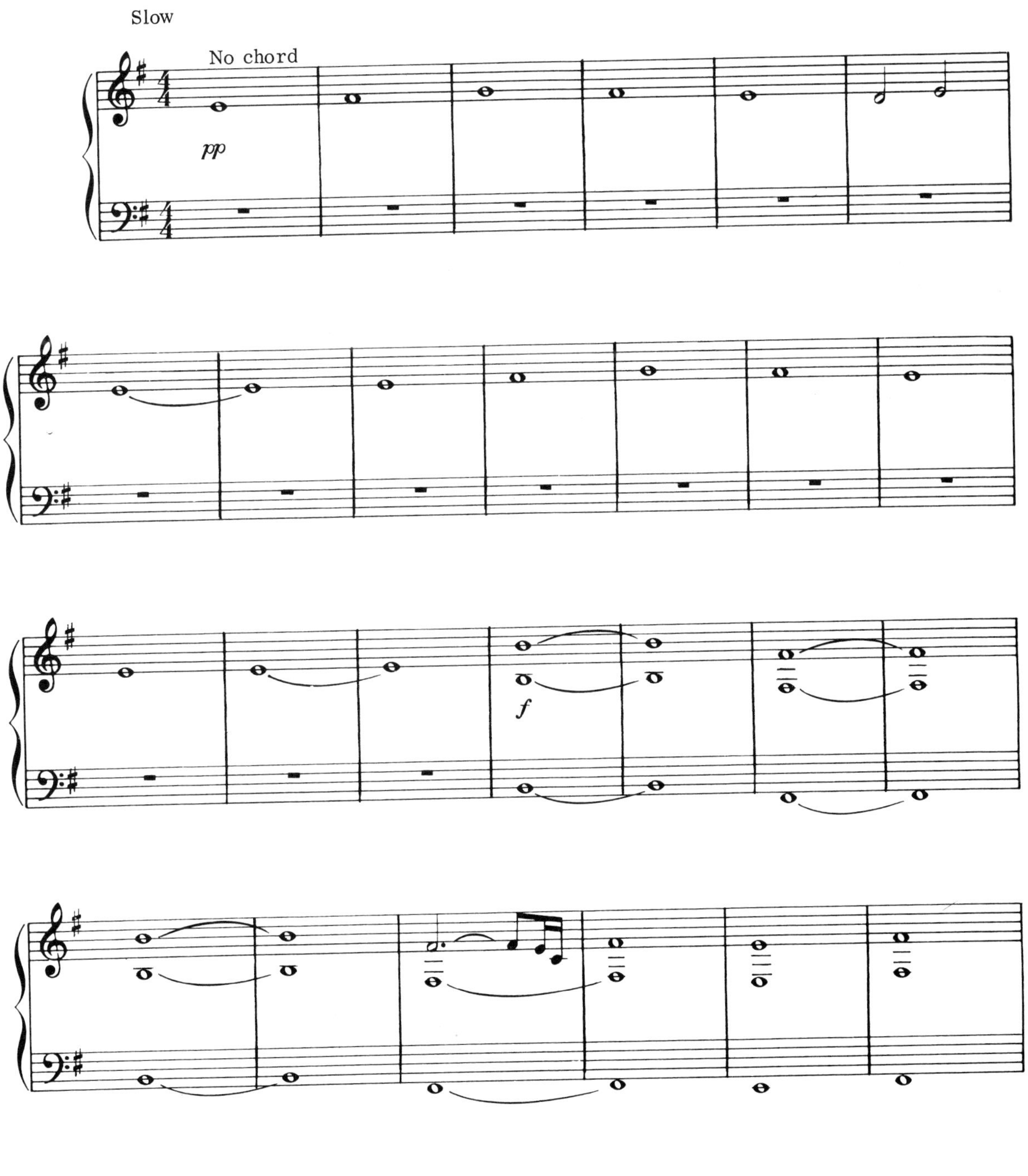

What shall we use — to fill — the emp-ty —
spa - ces — Where — we used to talk? —
How shall I fill the fi-nal — pla - ces?
How should I — com - plete the wall? —

Young Lust

Words & Music by
ROGER WATERS
& DAVID GILMOUR

Am
G
Ooh, I need a dir-ty wom-an;
Am
Em
Ooh I need a dir-ty girl.
Will some wo-man in this des-ert land
make me feel like a real man?
Take this rock 'n' roll re-fu-gee,
A
Em
G
Ooh babe, set me free.

Em
Am
Ooh,
G
I need a dir- ty wo-man;
Am
Ooh,
Em
I need a dir-ty girl.
F
F#
Em
G

Am7
G
Am7
Em
Am
Ooh — I need a dir-ty
G
wo-man;
Am
Ooh, — I need a dir-ty
Em
girl. —
Em
Repeat and fade

One of my turns

Words & Music by
ROGER WATERS

Em
F
C
can feel—— one of my turns com-ing on.
F
C
Em
Dm
I feel—— cold as a
F
G
raz - or blade, Tight as a tour - ni - quet, Dry as a fun - er - al drum.
A Tempo
E♭
B♭
E♭
B♭
C7
f
Run to the bed—— room, in the suit-case on the left—— You'll find my
rall.
f
Dm
E♭
fav - our - ite axe.——
Don't look so fright-

Eb
Bb
Dm
— ened, This is just a pass-ing phase, — One of my bad days. —
Bb
Eb
Bb
— Would you like to watch— T. V.? —— Or
Eb
Bb
Dm
get be-tween— the sheets?— Or con - tem - plate the si - lent free - way? Would you
Eb
like some-thing to eat? —— Would you like to learn— to fly? ——
Dm
Would you?— Would you like to see— me try?

D
G
C
G
E♭
B♭
E♭
B♭
Dm
E♭
B♭
E♭
B♭
Dm
Am7
Dm7
C
E♭
Would you like to call— the cops?—— Do you think it's time— I stopped-
Gm
Why are you run - ning a - way?——

Don't Leave me now

Words & Music by
ROGER WATERS

D♭maj7
B♭11
How could you go
When you
know how I need you, need you, need you,
G
G+
To beat to a pulp on a Sat-urday night? Oh,
E+
babe, —— Don't leave me now.
D♭maj7
How can you treat me this
B♭maj9
way? Run-ning a - way.
G
Oh, babe, Why are you running a-way? —
3 times
Dm
Am
Dm
F
G
Am
Ooh ——
(lh) (lh)

Another Brick in the Wall: part 3.

Words & Music by
ROGER WATERS

G
an - y-thing — at all.
Oh, no,
Dm
Don't think I'll need an-y-thing at all.
F
C
All in all— it was all just bricks in the
Dm
wall.
F
All in all— you were
C
all just bricks in the
Dm
wall.
Repeat and fade

Goodbye Cruel World

Words & Music by
ROGER WATERS

Hey you

Words & Music by
ROGER WATERS

Bm
Am
Em
Don't give in with-out a fight.
Dm
Em
Hey you! Out there on your own Sit-ting
Bm
Em
na-ked by the 'phone, Would you touch me?
Hey you! With your
Bm
ear a-gainst the wall, Wait-ing for some-one to call out, Would you touch me?
D
D7
G
D
C
Hey you! — Would you help me to car-ry the stone?
f

Bm
Am
Em
O-pen your heart,
I'm com-ing home.
Am
Em
Am
Em
Am
Em
C
D
G
D
C
But it was on-ly fan-ta-sy,

G D C
The wall was too high as you can see. No
D G D C
mat-ter how he tried he could not break free And the
D7 Em Dm
worms ate in-to his brain.
Em Dm Em
Dm Em

Dm
Em
Hey, you! Out there on the road, Always
Bm
C
Em
do - ing what you're told, Can you help me? Hey you! Out
Bm
there be-yond the wall, Break-ing bot - tles in the hall, Can you help me?
D
D7
G
D
C
Hey you! Don't tell me there's no hope at all.
Bm
Am
Em
To - geth - er we stand, Di - vid - ed we fall.

Is there anybody out there?

Words and Music by
ROGER WATERS

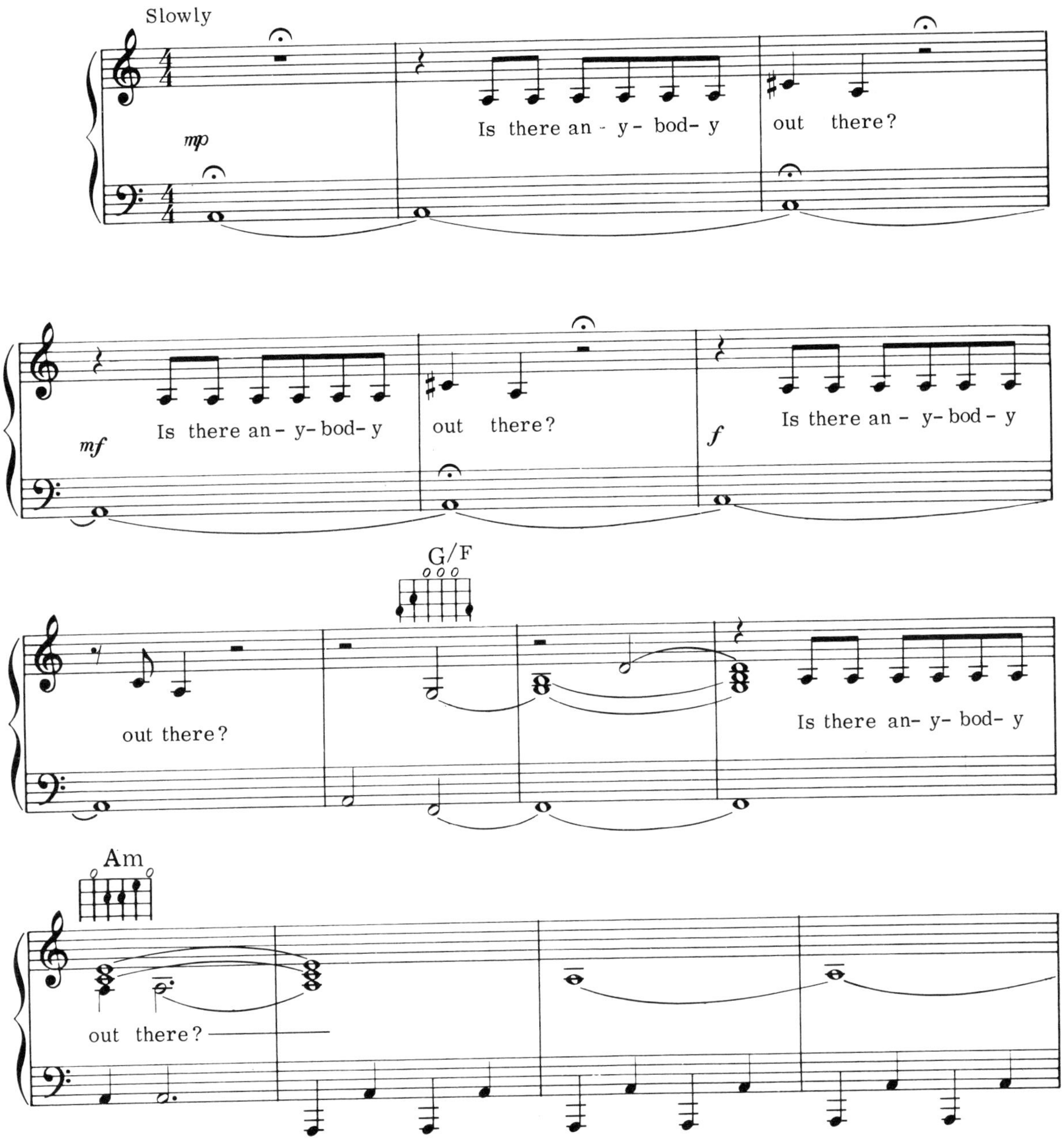

Am
Am6
mf
Am
Am6
Am

C
Am
C
Am
mf
Am6
Am
rall.

Nobody Home

Words and Music by
ROGER WATERS

C7
I've got e - lec-tric light
And I've got sec-ond
F
Fm
C
E7
sight. I've got a - maz-ing pow-ers of ob - serv - a-tion
Am
D7
G
E7
Am
And that is how I know
When I try to get
C+
C6
C
D
through
On the tel-ephone to you
Fm6
C
F
C
There'll be no-bo-dy home.

F
C
E
I've got the ob- lig-a-to-ry— Hendrix perm—— And the in- ev- i- ta-ble— pin-hole
3
f
E7+
F
C
burns All down the front of my fav-our-ite sa-tin shirt.——
F
C
E
I've got nic- o-tine stains on my fin-gers,—— I've got a sil-ver spoon on a
F
C
3
chain.—— I've got a grand pi- an- o to prop up my mor-tal re- mains.——
C7
I've got wild star-ing eyes And I've got a strong urge to

F
Fm
C
E
fly
But I've got no-where to fly to, (fly to,
Am
D7
G
E7
Am
fly to, fly to.)
Oooh
Babe,
C
D7
Fm6
when I pick up the phone
There's still no-bo-dy
mp
C
F
C
F
home.
I've got a
mf
C
E
E7
pair of Go-hill's boots
But I got fad-ing roots.
mp

Vera

Words and Music by
ROGER WATERS

Am
D
G
C
Em
G
Ve - ra!
Ve - ra!
D
What has be-come of you?
Em
C
Does an - y - bod - y else in here
D
G
D/F♯
C
Feel the way I do?
Em

Bring the boys back home

Words and Music by
ROGER WATERS

Comfortably Numb

Words and Music by
DAVID GILMOUR
and ROGER WATERS

Just the ba— sic facts——Can you show me where – it hurts?— There is no pain, you are re-ced-
—— ing.—— A dis— tant ship smoke on the ho – ri-zon,——
You are on- ly com— ing through—in waves. Your lips move but I can't hear what you're
say-ing. When I was a child – I had a fe- ver. My
hands felt— just like two bal-loons. Now I've got— that feel— ing once a-gain.

G
C
G
I can't explain, you would not un-der-stand. This is not how I am.
A
C
G
D
I have be-come com-fort-a-bly numb.
A
D
A
C
G
3
C
G
A
D
I, I,

C G D Bm
I have be-come com-fort'bly numb. O. K., O. K., O. K. Just a lit-tle
A G Em Bm
pin-prick. There'll be no more aaah! But you may feel a lit-tle sick. Can you
A G
stand up? I do believe it's work-ing. good! That-'ll keep you go-ing through the show. Come
Bm D A
on, it's time to go. There is no pain, you are re - ced - ing.
D A C
A dis-tant ship smoke on the ho - ri - zon. You are on- ly com- ing through- in

G
C
G
waves. Your lips move but I can't hear—what you're say— ing. When
D
A
D
I——was a child— I—caught a fleeting glimpse
Out of the cor- ner of my
A
C
G
eye.
I turned— to look— but it—was gone. I cannot put— my fin— ger on—
C
G
A
— it now.— The child is grown,— The dream is gone—
And——
C
G
D
I have be-come Com-fort-'bly numb.——

The Show must go on.

Words and Music by
ROGER WATERS

Cmaj7
There must be some mis-take, I did-n't mean to let them Take a-way my
G C G
soul. Am I too old? Is it too late?
D G C G
Ooh Ma, Ooh Pa! Where has the feel-ing gone?
D G C
Ooh Ma, Ooh Pa! Will I re-mem-ber the songs?
D G C Gsus/C G
Ooh ah! The show must go on!

In the Flesh

Words and Music by
ROGER WATERS

Moderately Slow
No chord

A
Bm
C♯m7
E
A
So ya Thought ya
D
A
Might like to Go to the show.—
To feel the warm
D
A
thrill of con-fu-sion, That space ca-det glow.
I've got some bad
Bm
news for you, sun-shine. Pink is-n't well.— He stayed back at the ho-tel And they've

C♯m
E
sent us a - long as a sur - ro - gate band. We're going to find out where you
A
fans real - ly stand. Are there an - y queers in the thea - tre to - night? Get 'em
D
A
up a - gainst the wall. Get them! There's one in the spot - light He don't
D
look right to me. Get him up a - gainst the wall. Get them! And
A
Bm
that one looks Jewish And that one's a coon. Who let all this riff raff

Bm6
Bm7
C♯m
in - to the room? There's one smok - ing a joint And an -
E
- oth - er with spots. If I had my way I'd have all of them
A
No chord
shot.
rall.

Run like Hell.

Words & Music by
DAVID GILMOUR
& ROGER WATERS

D
run, run, run, run, run, run, run, run,
run, run. You bet-ter
Em
make your face up in your fav-our-ite-dis-guise— with your
run all day and run all— night— and
(Instrumental on 𝄋)
F
but-ton down lips and your roll-er blind— eyes,— with your
keep your dir-ty feel-ings deep in— side,— and if you're
Em
emp-ty smile— and your
tak-ing your girl— friend
hun-gry heart— Feel the
out to-night—you'd bet-ter
C
bile ris— ing from your guil-ty past,— with your
park the car— well out of sight,— 'cause if they
B
nerves in tat-ters as the cock-le-shell— shat—ters and the
catch you in the back seat tryin' to pick her——locks—they're gon-na
E
ham-mers bat-ter
send you back to moth-er in a

TO CODA
D
down your door, — you bet - ter run.
card-board box, — you bet - ter run.
1.
2.
D.S. al CODA
CODA
5 times
Dm
3
D
A/D
G
D
A/D
G
rall. . . . .
D

Waiting for the Worms.

Words & Music by
ROGER WATERS

G
C
G
worms — to come.
In per-fect i - sol-a— tion
C
G
Am
here be-hind my wall.
Wait-ing for the
G
C
worms — to come.
Am
G
Am
C
Wait - ing to cut out the dead wood,
Wait - ing to clean up the ci - ty,
Am
G
Am
G
Wait - ing to fol - low the worms.
Wait - ing to put on a black shirt,

Am
Wait - ing to weed out the weak- lings, Wait - ing to smash in their win-dows And
G Am G
kick in their doors, Wait - ing for the fi - nal so - lu-tion To streng-then the strain,
Am G Am
Wait - ing to fol - low the worms, Wait - ing to turn on the show-ers And
G Am G
fire — the ov-ens, Wait - ing for the queens and the coons And the reds and the Jews,
Am G Am
Wait - ing to fol - low — the worms.

G
C
G
Would you like to see — Bri - tan - nia rule — a - gain — my
C
Bm
Am
G
friend?
All you have to do is fol - low — the worms.
Em
G
Would you like to send our
G7
C
G
C
col - oured cou - sins home a - gain, — my friend?
Am
G
Em
D/E
Repeat and fade
All you need to do is fol - low — the worms.

Stop

Words & Music by
ROGER WATERS

The Trial

Words & Music by
ROGER WATERS
& BOB EZRAM

Em
F♯
I al-ways said he'd come to no good in the end, your honour. If they'd let me have my way I could have
Em
G
G♯o
flayed him in-to shape. But my hands were tied. The bleed-ing hearts and ar-tists let him
D
Em7-5
Em
get a-way—with mur-der, let me ham-mer him to-day. Cra - zy toys in the at—tic, I am
rall. . . . . .
a tempo
Bmaj7
B
F♯m
D
cra - zy, tru-ly gone fish-ing. They must have tak-en my mar—
D♯o
Em7-5
Em
Bmaj7
B
—bles a - way.— Cra - zy, toys in the at—tic, he is cra - zy.

Em
(Call the defendant's wife)
You lit - tle shit you're in it now, I hope they throw a - way the
F
key, you should have talked to me more of-ten than you did but no, you
Em
had to go your own way, have you
brok-en an-y homes up late-ly?
C
Just five min-utes, worm, your hon-our,
B
him and me a - lone.
Em7-5
babe!
F♯m
F♯
Come to moth-er, Ba-by, let me
Bm
hold you in my arms M'
G
lud I never wanted him to
G♯o
get in an-y trouble, why'd he
D
ev-er have to leave me?
Worm, your honour, let me take him home.
rall. . . . .

Em7-5 Em Bmaj7 B
Cra - zy, ov-er the rain— bow, I am cra - zy, bars in the win— dow,
a tempo
F♯m D D♯o
There must have been a door there in the wall, When I came
Em7-5 Em B maj7 B
in.
Cra - zy, ov-er the rain—bow, he is cra - zy, The
Em Am
ev-i-dence— be-fore the court is in-con-tro-ver-ti-ble, there's no need for the ju-ry to re -
Em
tire. In all my years of judg-ing I have nev-er heard be-fore of

Am
Em
some-one more de-ser-ving— the full pen-al-ty of law. The way you made them suf-fer, your ex-
Am
quis-ite wife and moth-er, Fills me with the urge to de-fec-ate.
Em
Am
Since, my friend, you have re-vealed your deep-est fear, I sen-tence you to be ex-posed be-
Em
Am
fore your peers. Tear down the wall!
Em
Am
Repeat and fade
8va basso
loco

Outside the Wall

Words & Music by
ROGER WATERS

**Published by Pink Floyd Music Publishers Ltd.,
27 Noel Street, London W1V 3RD.**

Exclusive Distributors:

Music Sales Limited
8/9 Frith Street,
London W1V 5TZ, England

Music Sales Corporation
24 East 22nd Street, New York,
NY 10010 USA.

Music Sales Pty. Limited
27 Clarendon Street, Artarmon,
Sydney NSW 2064 Australia.

ORDER NO. AM64205

Printed by Scotprint Ltd, Musselburgh, Scotland.

(UK) ISBN 0 7119 1031 6
(USA) ISBN 0 8256 1076 1

7/87